Something About...

Priscilla Fugah

BookLeaf
Publishing

India | USA | UK

Presentation by *BookLeaf Publishing*

Web: www.bookleafpub.com

E-mail: info@bookleafpub.com

ISBN: 9789360942076

First edition 2024

The Sun

The sun rises quicker
on the east side
when she lets you
stare directly into her eyes.
Unintentional,
the way she holds your gaze,
keeps you fixated upon her,
until hope leaves your body
and the energy is no more.
You seek to speak words to her,
to plead for more time,
but only air makes its way
from deep within you
and out through your lips.
Dry, chapped,
you're in need of water.
Speechless
and she in return
appears mute.
Both in silence,
you wait for something
to draw you out.
You wait for the right time.
You wait for
the alarm to chime

6 o clock, and
now you have a
different appointment.
Now you can
break your gaze.
Turn away from the window
Crawl out of bed
And start your day.
Again.

She thinks

She thinks in blue,
not of you
but in blue.
Of deep waters and tepid waves.
Of summer blues
and night time hues.
She thinks of a time not long ago
when she lost someone she once knew
in those navy sheets stained
by memory.

She thinks in pink
of how she likes to drink
and not long after, sing.
Of rosé and roses.
Thorns pressed to lips.
Of yours pressed to hers.
She thinks of bottles in hands
emptied and broken, sitting in sink
Of pills that were attached to pink in her drink
that one time.

She thinks in white
Of linen and that diet
she began 6 years ago but never stuck to.

Of lillies and thread counts.
Hotel rooms and hospital lights.
Of the ghosts of several pasts that haunt her
Men dressed in white
gaining her trust and then

She thinks in Red
Of anger and rage
Struggling to control.
Of blood counts and periods
How pain is always linked to red
And how red is sometimes brown,
Burgundy.

She thinks in colour of almost everything
Of how everything is linked to a colour
and that what you thought you could trust
you could never.
She thinks in colour
becuase its easier
Colours don't change
and colours remember
even when you can't.

When Winter Came

When winter came
We lost shelter
Lost home and hope
Warmth
We lost who we were
Lost youth and sprite
No longer new
Our family of four
Walked through old
Sat in cold
Rode in trucks that drove us through past
Slept in yesterday
In coats, blankets, newspaper, from a time
before
We climbed through antecendence
Crawled over something blue, something new,
borrowed, and...
Hid behind throwbacks and
Snuck around predecessors
Until finally no longer new
We shook off old like dust to the ground
Shrugged off memories
And "remember when"s
Took shelter on foreign land
In new hope and past resilience

When winter came
We lost who we were
And gained who we are

I Art

I scale trees in my spare time,
a new found talent.
Last winter I found out that I
am art.
No, not artist, art. Subject matter.
Still life, except animate.

Last winter I found out that
winter wasn't just a season,
or a few months, but a feeling.
I try not to read too much into it,
but I am art, I feel winter.

Last winter I found my old treasure chest.
I wish I'd found something better.
Just old journals and cheap trinkets
from several last winters ago.

Last winter I met an old friend,
rekindled with a past comfort blanket.
Somehow it feels warmer now than it
ever did, but I am winter, I feel art.
I tried not to read too much into it.

Last winter the old journal spoke to me.

Maybe I read too much into it, and
now we are hand in hand,
me and my comfort blanket,
me and my old friend.

Last winter I became art,
art became winter,
winter became me,
and I became an image of my past self,
alone at the bus stop,
waiting for summer.

I shook hands with the demon inside of me,

a reoccurring guest.
Said my greetings to the creature that controls
my life,
the formless being that dominates everything I
do.
Like a cloud above my head,
a ghost in my cupboard,
it never speaks, only stares.
I never knew silence could mean so much.
With weighted shackles upon my feet,
I sat down with my most hated foe.
I never asked its name,
but Fear never should've had a name to begin
with.

Furniture

At first I hadn't noticed
how I'd become immobile,
less important, inanimate.
I hadn't noticed I'd lost my place.
Maybe I was too self-absorbed,
too focused on making it through the day.
Maybe I should've told you I was having a hard time
That each morning was filled with regret,
each step heavier than the last,
but I didn't think friendships were so feeble,
or that we'd all drift apart whilst I was trying to survive
Maybe I didn't know what trust was,
maybe I did, I just couldn't trust you.
So I guess you could say it was my fault,
that when I spoke, no one responded,
and wooden frames began to fix me into place,
floral tapestry slowly adorned my body
and I was pushed into a corner and left in silence.

Imbalances

I speak to you of imbalances
Of black and white
Hot and cold.
The way the sun shines high on winter days
And your bowl burns up, but its contents are
cold.
You consider these domestic issues
Small things that matter only largely at home
If at all.
What about politics and the real problems in the
world
You once asked
But I daren't speak of those
Not one to bring the mood down
Or cast a rift between the fabric of our
relationship,
I keep the conversation simple.
I speak of colours, but not races,
The physical body, but not psyche.
I speak very few words on conspiracy theories.
Lets change the topic,
I always ask,
And you fail to adhere.
In earnest our conversations hold no depth,

Only surface based interactions for the most
part,
Lest we fall into the trap of talking deep and
thinking deep
And stumble upon the knife that's hacks away at
our relational fabric.
The knife that reminds us that we too closely
resemble the
Imbalances and inconsistencies
That are our domestic issues.

Watching you

Watching you,
I am aware of your rarity
Something that only my mind can imagine
Yet here you are in flesh and bones
Muscle and veins
I think of you a lot
I'm not sure whether you know this
You cross my mind
And then you stick
Like glue to paper
Like gum on jeans
I think of when we'd first met
Under the passageway
The train rattling above us
I was in a hurry, so naturally I tripped
"clumsy child"
Those were the words you'd whispered to
yourself after a short burst of laughter
Those are the words you still call me by
A sort of nickname if you will
I remember how you helped me up
Told me to be careful
And wished me luck to wherever I was going
You weren't aware that I'd needed it, but I had
I think about you now

And how you haven't changed
Frozen in your place like fruit in ice
Or a relic held in a museum preserving history
Each experience with you is slightly different,
but you're still the same
Always refreshing to see
Always a sight of amazement
I wonder if you know how much I marvel at you
I wonder if you know I'd be lost without you
Or how comforting it is to have you tuck me in
bed
Give me a goodnight kiss
And tell me the stories that you never had time
to tell me earlier in the day

Death

You, Death,
Follow me around for countless days
"Well, sometimes I'm busy."
Lest those days you're busy.
You speak few words of encouragement
Few words to make me go on
And more to make me stop.
Very often you tell me the worlds not made for
me
"Well, it's not"
You whisper it in my ear when the cold wind
hits
And the weather makes me shake.
On rainy days, you beat your drum inside my
head
Thump thump, thump thump
A step faster than the rain
A cause of migraine.
You make your presence known
Even on slower days
And on days where everything is just too much,
You never leave my side.
What a miserable comfort.
"Thanks."
I guess I'm saying your presence is too much

And the dark cloud over my head is overbearing,
Because you, death,
Follow me around for countless days

Confused

Birds on tree tops
I don't know how to say this
"whisper it"
I doubt that would help.
Lemons fall from the same tree that life does.
I don't know what that means.
"what are you trying to say?"
Words I guess,
Something to explain the situation,
To explain my feelings for you.
I've never rooted a carrot.
My mind is a mess.
Elephants on tree tops,
No.
Giraffes?
I guess I'm saying that's how you make me feel.
"A mess?"
No.
Yes,
Confused I mean.
"I don't know what you mean."
Elephants sit in waiting rooms
I'll sit and wait for you.
"What?"
I think it means I like you,

Maybe more than like
Definitely more than like.
A bunny hop to consciousness.
I think I mean I love you
I think I meant to say words that actually made
sense
But that's easier said than done.

Write

Sometimes I struggle to write,
And its not for a lack of being able to express myself,
Just an inability to make it make sense.
I write words on paper.
Start sentences and first lines,
But quite often I'm stuck behind two or three.
A catchy phrase and nothing more.
Lost on how to make it longer,
To turn into something more,
Into the deep, thought provoking piece I had imagined.
So sometimes I simply give up,
And I retire pieces of poems, sentences, phrases,
To the graveyard, hoping one day,
I'll revive the dead and give it new life.

The Right Thing

No one says,
the right thing.
I'm still coming to terms with that.
No one says,
what I want to hear.
Things like;
"I'm sorry,"
"I understand,"
"I love you."
Silence even,
accompanied by a hug.
No one says,
the right thing.
No one says it,
at the right moment,
and it makes no difference,
because I'm still sad,
and your words wont change that.

How can I?

How can I explain that I love you,
But don't want to be with you?
That I hate you,
But can't deal with the idea of having to be
without you.
That I think about you every minute of the day,
But that I wish I didn't.
How do I explain to you that too much of bad
thing isn't good,
And that to me, you're a bad thing?
That attachment doesn't always mean it's good,
Just signifies dependency.
How can I explain that I need time,
Space?
That I don't think this will work,
Even if we try.
How can I say all of this,
Without hurting your feelings?

Brown

The colour of your coffee
Sat in pot
Brewed to perfection
Ready to pour into your favourite mug
For the sixth day in a row.
You work by routine
Rigid almost in the way you think
The way you process.
You start at 6am.
Yawn
And crawl out of bed
Shower first, then coffee.
It's the only order that makes sense
To you.
On Saturdays you work at a slower pace
Not pushed by the need to be at work
To be a corporate body.
You stand in the shower longer than necessary
And let the water fall off of your body
And down the drain.
You step out, dry,
Then moisturise,
Dress for the day planned ahead.
You pour yourself a cup of coffee,
Stare at the sky,
And start your day.

Voice

On Monday, you lose your voice
Not sure when you lost it
Where.
You struggle to find it,
To regain something you only just lost.
You search as far back as Thursday,
But Thursday you still had your voice,
Still had the power to vocalise your thoughts,
That's not where you lost it.
Friday is no different.
You had your voice till the early hours,
Slurred by vodka shots and a chaser.
Drunk, home alone,
You screamed the words to every song you'd
ever heard.
Raspy was your voice on Saturday afternoon,
Slept in till late,
Stone on a grate,
But still, you had your voice
You had your voice.
You don't consider Saturday night.
Don't consider Sunday
You don't want to think about them,
You don't want to think in general,
But people are asking you questions

In a four walled room designed to make you
answer.
"What happened on that night?"
You ask yourself how you got here.
"Where was the last place you remember
being?"
How did you get here?
"We won't be able to get anywhere if you don't
tell us"
Why are you here?
"Do you remember?"
You remember, and open your mouth
But you can't say.
You remember faces
Actions.
You remember exactly what happened,
But the words won't leave your mouth.
On Saturday night you lost your voice,
Your ability to plead.
You lost yourself.
They found you on Sunday
You haven't been home since
But you know that's not where you lost it

You

Human in all that you do
Turn into an animal at night
Only hours after sunset
Your entire form changes

No longer human by your actions
You wait for a full moon
8 shots and a bottle of henny
You embrace the wildness

Now a growing monster
A habitual beast
You flail your hands about
Hit everything in your way
An eager madness

You
Human in all your after effects
Apologise for your actions
Repetitive speech
"It won't happen again" "I'm sorry"
Only a week later
Your apologies come to visit again
Barely healed
Still bruised

You whisper
"You're still so beautiful.
I love you"

You
A habitual liar
Never human
Take my hand at the alter
And make promises you can never keep

Gas Masks

You didn't think you'd need them when you first
learnt to breathe.
The airs never been clean, full of years of man
made fumes and carbon gasses,
But now it's debris and carcinogens.
Tank fuel and tear gas.
Pieces of what was, and what could've been
People who were, who no longer are.
Your country's never seen peace,
But I guess you were at peace.
Made do with the displeasure, discomfort, and
disapproval in the hopes of talking it out,
Negotiating a deal that would leave you
unscathed,
Would leave your cities as whole,
Independent and proud, owning what was yours
and living alongside others,
But other's were in displeasure, discomfort and
disapproval of yours being yours
And greed may have been the name for it but
fear is what they chose and fear is what they
present
But fear didn't bomb your city, people did,
And fear didn't keep the war going,
But fears what's brought out the masks,

Guns,
And fear's what made you grieve
Loss after loss.

Beauty

Find beauty in what's around you
And who you are
Just like how I found beauty in you
And who you make me be

www.ingramcontent.com/pod-product-compliance
Lightning Source LLC
LaVergne TN
LVHW021352200726
843509LV00014B/2814